Create Your

EPIC

EXECUTIVE
BRAND

a workbook for elevating your
presence, influence, and connectivity

Create Your
EPIC
EXECUTIVE BRAND

CAROL BERGERON

 Concord, MA

Copyright © 2026 Carol Bergeron. All rights reserved.

No part of this publication may be reproduced, stored in or introduced into a retrieval system, or transmitted, in any form, or by any means (electronic, digital, mechanical, photocopying, recording, or otherwise), without the prior written permission of the author, except as permitted by U.S. copyright law.

Published in the United States of America by:
Talent Magnet Series™, Concord, Massachusetts, www.TalentMagnetSeries.com

International Standard Book Number ISBN: 978-0-9887071-2-2

This publication is provided for educational and informational purposes. Different people may interpret the content in different ways, and the highlighted methods might not fit your specific situation. It is up to you to decide if, how, and to what extent you will apply the methods contained herein.

DEDICATION

This workbook is dedicated to executives and leaders
who dare to embrace their true selves,
chart distinctive paths toward meaningful impact,
and foster connections that help create a legacy.
I am honored to be part of your journey.

CONTENTS

- Using This Workbook 9
- About Executive Brands 10
- Why is an EPIC Executive Brand Important? 13
- Journey to Your EPIC Executive Brand 14
- PHASE 1: Who Are You Now? 15
- Canvas 1: What Experiences Have Shaped Your Leadership Style? 16
- Canvas 2: What Are Your Core Values? 19
- Canvas 3: In What Do You Excel? 23
- Canvas 4: What is Your Current Reputation? 24
- Canvas 5: What is the Unique Mix of Superpowers that Sets You Apart? 25
- PHASE 2: What Are Your Aspirations? 26
- Canvas 6: What Are Your Big, Bold Goals? 27
- Canvas 7: How Do You Want Others to Experience You in the Future? 28
- PHASE 3: Craft Your EPIC Executive Brand 29
- Canvas 8: Core Hallmarks of Your EPIC Executive Brand 30
- Sample Executive Brand Statements 31
- Canvas 9: Adapt Your Brand Statement 32
- Canvas 10: Your Biographical Narrative 33
- PHASE 4: Achieve Your EPIC Executive Brand 34
- Canvas 11: How Will You Achieve Your EPIC Executive Brand? 35
- Canvas 12: Workplace Engagement 37
- Canvas 13: Action Plan 39
- Congratulations 40
- About the Author & Coach 41

USING THIS WORKBOOK

This workbook is crafted to guide you in creating your EPIC executive brand. It serves as a central hub for capturing and documenting your ideas and decisions related to achieving desired new heights in your career and leadership legacy. It will engage your intellect, emotions, and senses to fuel the creation of a deep, rich, and authentic executive brand.

Upon completion of this journey, you will have developed:

- your unique, one-of-a-kind EPIC executive brand and its practical variations such as your elevator speech or self-introduction, a brief profile, and a full biographical narrative, and
- an action plan for lifting your visibility in your organization and industry.

As with any meaningful endeavor, the quality of the output depends on the quality and thoughtfulness of the input. Invest in yourself and the process.

Some questions you are asked will take little time to answer while others will warrant more reflection. The journey, while presented in a linear fashion, can be anything but. That is because executive brand design can be iterative in nature. Do not be surprised if finishing one reflection canvas leads you to refining a previous one. It is all part of the process.

Consider this workbook a catalyst for channeling your energy and passion into actionable output. Complete alongside a trusted colleague or small group of peers and benefit from testing out your executive brand in a safe, supportive environment before going live.

Creating your EPIC executive brand is not a one-time event but an ongoing journey as your brand will evolve with new experiences, learnings, and personal growth. Be sure to re-use this workbook, framework, and tools for refining your EPIC executive brand as it evolves.

Taking this journey is about helping you achieve new heights in your career and leadership legacy by living your authentic self every day. Enjoy!

And a special acknowledgement goes to Ellie Eckhoff. Thank you for being such an enthusiastic supporter in addition to providing valuable feedback!

ABOUT EXECUTIVE BRANDS

You have a reputation, whether you planned it or not. The remaining question is whether your existing reputation helps or hinders your desire to achieve new heights in your career and leadership legacy. And there are a few building blocks that precede your EPIC executive brand including your identity and personal brand.

Q: What do identity, personal brand, and executive brand have in common?

They are all grounded in the genuine you. By design they exemplify your presence and reputation consistently experienced by people you engage with. And they highlight your uniqueness and value.

Q: What is your identity?

Your identity consists of your values and beliefs, characteristics that make you you, self-perception, and the perceptions of others. It is deeply personal and shaped by experience.

Q: What is your personal brand?

Your personal brand evolves from your identity, emphasizing the unique expertise and talents that define your professional reputation.

Q: What is an executive brand?

A: Building on your personal brand, an executive brand is a vibrant reflection of your authentic self. It showcases the work you do best, the complex problems you help solve, the positive impact you make, and the everyday experiences people have when engaging with you. It factors in your beliefs, values,

---

EXAMPLE

Identity: I am a person of integrity, strong work ethic, and curiosity who is passionate about developing oncology therapeutics.

Personal Brand: I'm a life science entrepreneur in oncology drug development and leader known for mentoring and developing others on the best practices of innovative, high-performance research teams.

Executive Brand: As a visionary entrepreneur with deep scientific expertise in oncology drug development and advancement, I'm recognized for repeatedly driving new therapeutics to market, cultivating a research environment rich in curiosity, collaboration, and innovation, developing a pipeline of scientific leaders, and prioritizing patient wellbeing.

expertise and leadership qualities, thoughtfully presented to elevate your professional reputation within your organization and across your industry. By connecting your executive brand with your organization's values and goals, you are empowered to inspire and lift others, build meaningful relationships, and create lasting value for yourself and those around you.

Q: How does creating an executive brand help you?

A: It helps you understand yourself better and prompts alignment of your beliefs, values, and goals with those of your organization. You will connect with others more genuinely by highlighting what makes encounters with you unique. It builds your credibility.

As a marketing tool for your career, it increases your value and visibility within your organization and industry. It can help you secure new projects, jobs, promotions, or roles like board advisor or director. Additionally, it positions you as a thought leader through activities like speaking and blogging, resulting in attracting new people, expanding your network, and broadening your impact.

Q: How does your executive brand help your organization?

A: For your organization, your executive brand can improve the workplace culture, contribute to drawing in new talent, enhance the image of the company and its products, as well as promote its brand overall.

Q: When is an executive brand used?

A: A well-prepared executive brand provides focus for all your encounters and choices. Your authenticity shows up in verbal, non-verbal, written communications, as well as all face-to-face and online exchanges.

Create Your EPIC Executive Brand

In summary, your EPIC executive brand consists of your unique combination of:

The work you do exceptionally well
+ the impact you want to have and on whom

Superpowers that shape how you go about doing your work
- *Deeply held beliefs & values*
- *Subject matter expertise*
- *Talents & Leadership qualities*

Alignment and connectivity with your organization
- *Professional role & goals*
- *What you stand for*
- *Mutual values*

Engagement - consistently shows up in your authentic interactions with others

Written, Verbal & Non-Verbal:
- *In-person*
- *On-line*

WHY IS AN EPIC EXECUTIVE BRAND IMPORTANT?

Why does it matter?

- It is your reputation
- You already have one, by default or by design

What's the value to you?

- Achieves clarity on you
- Aligns with your bold professional goals
- Engagement with others is consistently authentic
- Distinguishes and shares your uniqueness
- Strengthens your credibility
- Serves as a powerful career marketing tool:
  - Elevates your value and visibility in your organization and industry
  - Helps in landing a new project, job, promotion, role (i.e. board advisor or director)
  - Branching out into thought leadership (i.e. speaking, blogging)
  - Attracts people and grows your network

When & how is it used?

In all interactions:

- Professional, personal, and always authentic
- Written, verbal, and non-verbal
- In-person, meetings, and on-line

What's the value to your organization?

- Attracts new talent
- Enhances image of the company and its products
- Promotes company brand

TIP

Your executive brand evolves with new experiences and learnings so retain your work for future updates.

JOURNEY TO YOUR EPIC EXECUTIVE BRAND

Embark on the four-phase journey to

Elevate your Presence, Influence, and Connectivity

to heighten your career and leadership legacy.

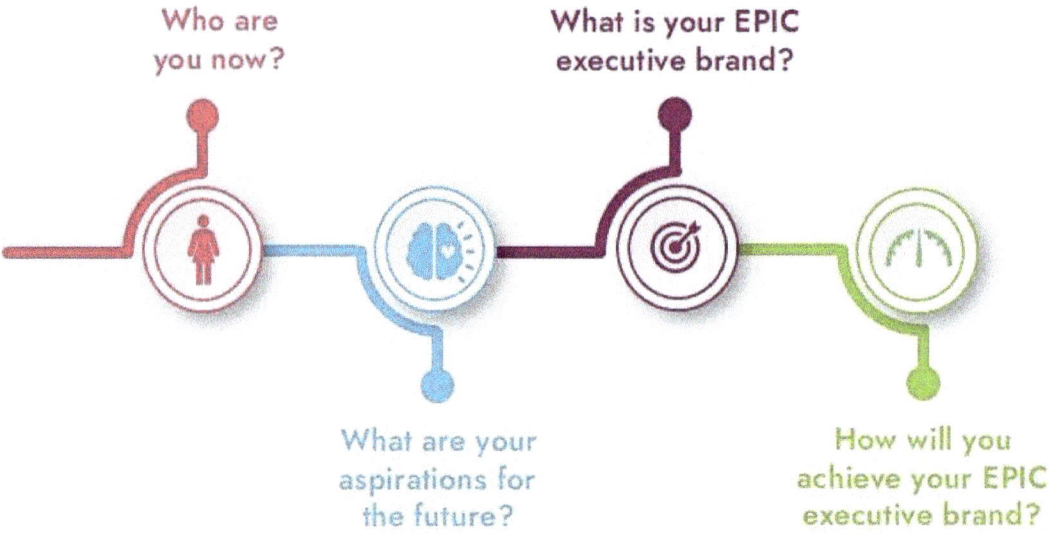

PHASE 1: WHO ARE YOU NOW?

Questions you will be asked to reflect on include:

1. What experiences have shaped your leadership style?
2. What are your core values?
3. What work do you do exceptionally well? What impact do you have and on whom?
4. What are your key talents and leadership qualities?
5. What is your current reputation? How do others see you?
6. What is the unique mix of superpowers that sets you apart?

Create Your EPIC Executive Brand

Canvas 1: What Experiences Have Shaped Your Leadership Style?

Your leadership style has been shaped through important experiences and relationships throughout your life. By thoroughly exploring the significant highs and lows you have encountered, including notable accomplishments, influential individuals, and the communities you have engaged with, you gain insight into the factors that have formed your approach to leadership as well as your perspectives, values, and the way you interact with others.

1. Identify pivotal moments, achievements, setbacks, influential people, and communities over your life and plot the most profound positive and negative experiences along the timeline.

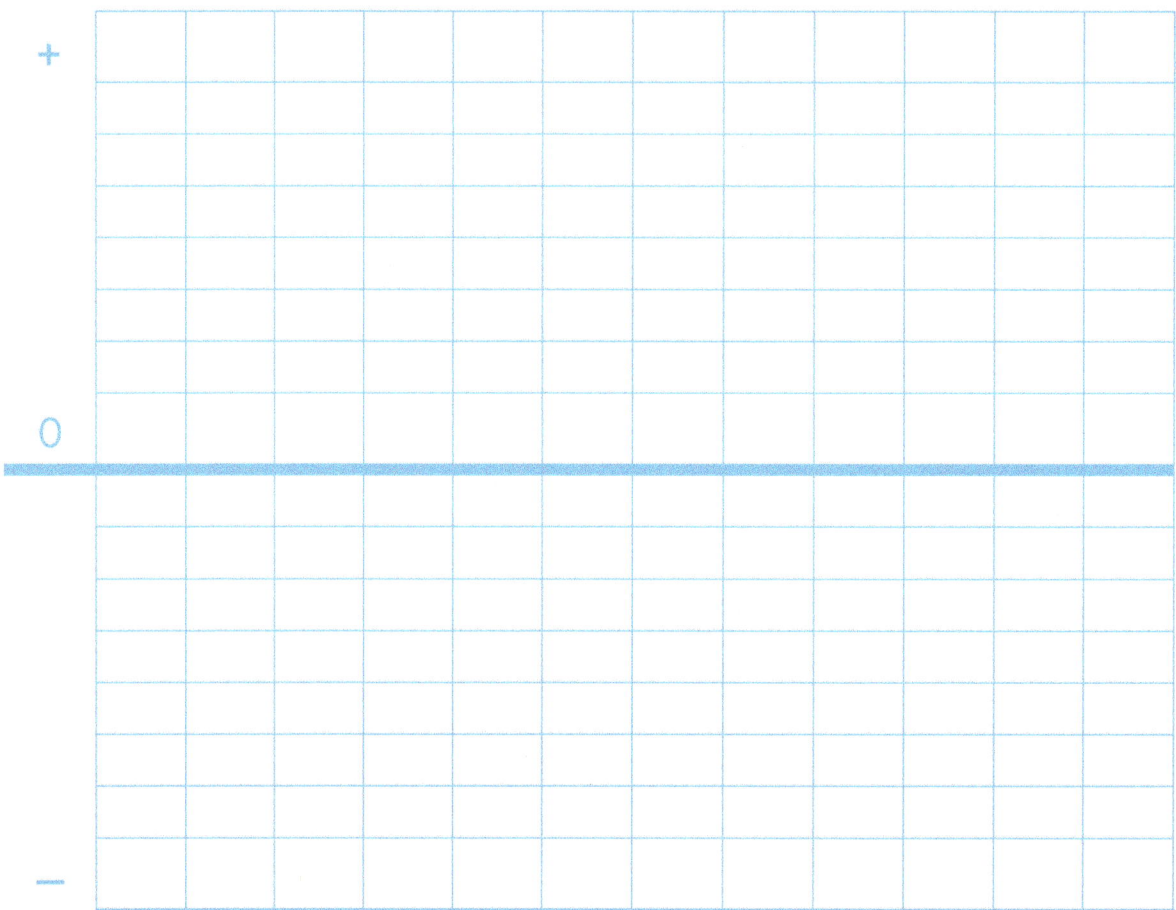

2. From your timeline, write a brief letter from your 100-year-old self to your younger self. Highlight pivotal moments and their significance and influence on your growth as a leader.

3. From the influences on your growth as a leader, make a list of the beliefs you hold about success. Then summarize how you define success.

4. From your insights, break your life story into chapters shaped by major transitions or turning points. Note what you learned, how you grew, and how the turning points influenced your leadership style.

> **TIP**
>
> The more specifics and personal stories you include, the deeper your insights and growth will be.

Canvas 2: What Are Your Core Values?

Core values tend to endure over time. That said, their prioritization, emphasis, and how they show up in different life situations can vary based on factors like people, goals, environment, and life stage. Treasure your current values, as they profoundly shape your personal and professional conduct and inform your beliefs, attitudes, decisions, actions, and how you engage with others.

1. From the list of values, select those of greatest importance to you. Add your own if not listed.

- ❏ Accountability
- ❏ Achievement
- ❏ Action
- ❏ Adaptability
- ❏ Advancement
- ❏ Adventure
- ❏ Aesthetics
- ❏ Affiliation
- ❏ Ambition
- ❏ Authenticity
- ❏ Authority
- ❏ Autonomy
- ❏ Awareness
- ❏ Balance
- ❏ Beauty
- ❏ Belonging
- ❏ Career
- ❏ Caution
- ❏ Challenge
- ❏ Change
- ❏ Collaboration
- ❏ Commitment
- ❏ Communication
- ❏ Community
- ❏ Compassion
- ❏ Competence
- ❏ Competition
- ❏ Cooperation
- ❏ Courage
- ❏ Creativity
- ❏ Curiosity
- ❏ Determination
- ❏ Development
- ❏ Dignity
- ❏ Discipline
- ❏ Diversity
- ❏ EQ
- ❏ Empathy
- ❏ Empowerment
- ❏ Energy
- ❏ Enjoyment
- ❏ Ethics
- ❏ Excellence
- ❏ Excitement
- ❏ Expression
- ❏ Fairness
- ❏ Faith
- ❏ Family
- ❏ Financial stability
- ❏ Fitness
- ❏ Flexibility
- ❏ Forgiveness
- ❏ Freedom
- ❏ Friendship
- ❏ Fulfillment
- ❏ Fun
- ❏ Future focus
- ❏ Happiness
- ❏ Harmony
- ❏ Health
- ❏ Home
- ❏ Honesty
- ❏ Hope
- ❏ Humility
- ❏ Humor
- ❏ Impact
- ❏ Inclusion
- ❏ Independence
- ❏ Influence
- ❏ Initiative
- ❏ Innovation
- ❏ Integrity
- ❏ Intuition
- ❏ Job security
- ❏ Joy
- ❏ Justice
- ❏ Kindness
- ❏ Knowledge
- ❏ Leadership
- ❏ Learning
- ❏ Legacy
- ❏ Leisure
- ❏ Liveliness
- ❏ Love
- ❏ Loyalty
- ❏ Meaning
- ❏ Mindfulness
- ❏ Multi-generational
- ❏ Nature
- ❏ Nurture
- ❏ Openness
- ❏ Optimism
- ❏ Order
- ❏ Parental
- ❏ Passion
- ❏ Patience
- ❏ Patriotism
- ❏ Peace
- ❏ Perseverance
- ❏ Personal growth
- ❏ Positivity
- ❏ Power
- ❏ Pride
- ❏ Privacy
- ❏ Recognition
- ❏ Reflection
- ❏ Relationships
- ❏ Reliability
- ❏ Religion
- ❏ Reputation
- ❏ Resilience
- ❏ Resourceful
- ❏ Respect
- ❏ Responsibility
- ❏ Results
- ❏ Risk taking
- ❏ Safety
- ❏ Security
- ❏ Serenity
- ❏ Service
- ❏ Simplicity
- ❏ Spirituality
- ❏ Sportsmanship
- ❏ Stability
- ❏ Status
- ❏ Stewardship
- ❏ Success
- ❏ Support
- ❏ Teamwork
- ❏ Thrift
- ❏ Time
- ❏ Tradition
- ❏ Tranquility
- ❏ Transparency
- ❏ Travel
- ❏ Trust
- ❏ Truth
- ❏ Understanding
- ❏ Uniqueness
- ❏ Usefulness
- ❏ Vision
- ❏ Vulnerability
- ❏ Wealth
- ❏ Wellbeing
- ❏ Wholeheartedness
- ❏ Wisdom
- ❏ _____
- ❏ _____
- ❏ _____
- ❏ _____
- ❏ _____

2. From the values chosen in step 1, organize related values into five clusters on the matrix. Give each cluster a name, meaningful definition, and symbol. These are your core values.

Clustered Values	Cluster Name	Definition	Symbol
· Learning · Personal growth · Knowledge · Wisdom	· Lifelong Learning	· the pursuit of lifelong learning & growth	💡
1			
2			
3			
4			
5			

3. Which of your core values align with those of your organization?

4. What additional insights surfaced from this reflection?

Cause4Pause: Navigating Misalignment of Values

As you develop your EPIC executive brand, you may realize that your core values do not fully align with those of your organization. This misalignment can arise for various reasons, such as shifts in your own values, limited communication about values during recruitment, changes in organizational leadership or ownership, shifts in strategic vision, and discrepancies between the organization's stated and actual values.

When encountering values misalignment, it can be helpful to reflect on the extent of the differences and how they play out in terms of your work experiences, impact, and feelings. With sufficient values' overlap, where you feel good about the work you do and its impact, you may find that you are right where you should be.

However, if the gaps feel significant and lead to routine distress, it may be time to explore other options.

One option is to focus on aligning values within your immediate team, especially on your values that do coincide with those of the organization. This may be enough for a solid foundation to move forward.

Another option is to initiate constructive conversations with other executives about revisiting the organization's values. Conversations that pair organizational values with strategic visioning and planning work well as organizational values are intended to support the achievement of strategic goals.

If the previous options are unsuitable and you experience a persistent mismatch between your values and those of the organization, it may be helpful to reflect on how this affects your experience and consider what environment will support you, your growth, and impact.

There is no one right answer. You will need to sift through the messiness and pay close attention to the extent of the gaps and your emotional response, day-to-day experience, ability to make impact, and career trajectory at the organization when forming your next steps.

Canvas 3: In What Do You Excel?

1. Reflect on examples of work you do exceptionally well. For each, place it under the relevant column such as moments of fulfillment, outstanding performance, or deep immersion. Ensure each column has at least one entry.
2. Answer the questions for each entry, noting your work, problems you solved, who benefited, what you enjoyed most, and the talents & leadership qualities that contributed to success.

Questions	Time(s) when you felt the most fulfilled.	Time(s) when you were amazed by how well you did the work.	Time(s) when fully immersed in the work and time just flew by.
What work were you doing? What problems were you solving?			
For whom did you do the work? How did they benefit?			
What about the work did you most enjoy? What feelings did it ignite in you?			
Of the talents & leadership qualities used, which contributed most to your success?			

Canvas 4: What is Your Current Reputation?

1. Gather feedback from work colleagues, managers, customers, partners, family, and friends to understand your current reputation; ask for specific examples and stories.

2. Summarize insights from personality tests, 360 feedback, and performance reviews, noting strengths and blind spots.

3. Highlight the strengths with the greatest potential when creating your EPIC executive brand.

Canvas 5: What is the Unique Mix of Superpowers that Sets You Apart?

A superpower is a strength that has been mastered over time and experience. While a strength has the potential to become a superpower with unwavering commitment to excel.

This reflection asks you to define the unique mix of superpowers by reviewing your completed canvases and noting:

- key insights from your life story,
- core values that align with your organization,
- work where you excel and make an impact,
- expertise, talents, and leadership qualities, and
- feedback from others and how they perceive you.

Begin to identify and define the unique mix of superpowers that sets you apart from others.

EXAMPLE

If your canvases reveal that you consistently inspire teams and drive innovation, your superpowers might include visionary leadership and creative problem-solving.

PHASE 2: WHAT ARE YOUR ASPIRATIONS?

More questions to think about:

7. What are your big, bold goals?

8. How do you want others to experience you in the future?

9. What will your superpowers be?

Create Your EPIC Executive Brand

Canvas 6: What Are Your Big, Bold Goals?

Setting big, bold, long-term, aspirational goals fuels intent, provides focus, and affords lead time to transform strengths into superpowers in support of your goals.

1. Capture your five most important goals.
2. Identify goals that align with those of your organization.

Canvas 7: How Do You Want Others to Experience You in the Future?

With your goals top of mind, describe:

- the experiences and feelings you want people to have when engaging with you,
- your unique superpowers = existing ones + strengths you will master over time, and
- approaches for transforming existing strengths into future superpowers.

How do you want others to experience you in all future interactions?	What will be your unique mix of superpowers now and in the future?	How will you transform existing strengths into future superpowers?

PHASE 3: CRAFT YOUR EPIC EXECUTIVE BRAND

Phase 3 brings together all your work in the form of your EPIC executive brand including:

10. The core hallmarks of your EPIC executive brand

11. A brief elevator speech used for self-introduction

12. A short profile

13. An expanded biographical narrative

Canvas 8: Core Hallmarks of Your EPIC Executive Brand

Characteristics of your EPIC executive brand include:
- It's big, bold, inspirational, and one-of-a-kind,
- captures the work at which you excel and are passionate,
- conveys your motivations for doing your work through the lens of your stakeholders,
- articulates a picture of what you want to create,
- highlights your unique mix of superpowers that people will come to expect, and
- is completely and authentically you!

Sample format:

> I am a [insert role(s)] and am passionate about [insert the work you do and/or causes] because it fuels my contributions and impact on [insert what you want to create and for whom]. In doing this important work and in all interactions, I uphold the values of [insert values] and leverage my natural talents of [insert superpowers].

Craft your initial EPIC executive brand in brief below.

Sample Executive Brand Statements

"As a biopharma executive, I champion breakthrough science and digital innovation to accelerate drug discovery and deliver transformative therapies. Guided by integrity, innovation, and collaboration, I elevate patient outcomes and inspire teams to achieve excellence."

- Biopharma Executive

"As an engineering executive driving disruption and innovation, I have led development of a next-generation avionic system that boosted customer engagement by 30 percent. By focusing on creativity, collaboration, and uncompromising safety and quality principles, we have successfully turned complex problems into elegant, reliable, and marketable solutions."

- Engineering Executive

"I translate complex cybersecurity threats into actionable protection strategies by leveraging AI-driven threat analysis and collaborating cross-functionally with compliance teams that have resulted in reducing fraud by 30% for financial institutions navigating ever evolving compliance requirements."

- Industry Solution Specialist

"I am a business development leader who leverages data-driven insights to identify new opportunities and employs creative negotiation strategies to broker strategic partnerships that have transformed competitors into collaborators. Through these efforts, I have increased annual revenue by 30 percent and expanded our presence across three new markets."

- Business Development Executive

"As an entrepreneur with a proven track record in international business, I have successfully launched three brands in Asia and Europe, increasing market share by 25% within the first year. I specialize in taking brands global, navigating cross-cultural challenges, and unlocking new markets by leveraging my strategic approach and global network."

- Global Business Leader

"As a recognized leader in organization and leadership development, I help individuals, teams, and organizations turn trying transitions into triumphs. Renowned for my strategic mindset, collaborative spirit, and self-discovery coaching approach, I guide people to unlock their strengths and aspirations, navigate unique paths forward, and achieve meaningful, lasting outcomes."

- Leadership & Transition Coach

Canvas 9: Adapt Your Brand Statement

This section focuses on presenting your EPIC executive brand across diverse settings. By considering the context and audience, you can ensure your brand message remains consistent, impactful, and true to what makes you you. Whether introducing yourself at an industry conference, updating your online profile, or sharing your narrative in written communications, tailoring your message helps you connect authentically while maintaining professionalism and approachability.

1. Craft your brief elevator speech or self-introduction for use at a professional event such as an industry conference.

2. Craft your brief professional profile for use on social media.

Canvas 10: Your Biographical Narrative

Compose a full biographical narrative suitable for posting on your organization's website or distributing at an industry speaking engagement. Begin with your brief profile from Canvas 9, then weave in key accomplishments, pivotal chapters or elements from your life story, expertise, superpowers and values. Make your narrative memorable by showcasing the complex problems you solve, your impact and growth. Continue to iterate until it's a story you'd be proud to share.

PEOPLE WITH REMARKABLE EXECUTIVE BRANDS

Warren Buffet
Caitlan Clark
Bill Gates
Melinda French Gates
Arianna Huffington
Michelle Obama
Reshma Saujani
Oprah Winfrey

PHASE 4: ACHIEVE YOUR EPIC EXECUTIVE BRAND

The more genuine your EPIC executive brand, the easier it becomes to navigate daily interactions, whether in one-to-one conversations, team meetings, or outreach efforts.

In this phase, you will answer questions like:

14. How will you achieve your EPIC executive brand?

15. How will you show up at work?

16. How will you monitor progress?

Create Your EPIC Executive Brand

Canvas 11: How Will You Achieve Your EPIC Executive Brand?

In general, how will you achieve your EPIC executive brand?

What approaches will you use inside and outside your organization?	What specific paths will you activate for outreach?	How will you monitor progress?

Sample Approaches
- Writing
- Publishing
- Speaking
- Volunteering
- Other_____

Sample Paths
- All interactions: 1-to-1s, team meetings
- As ally, mentor, sponsor
- Social media platforms
- Industry blogs, podcasts, conferences
- Professional associations
- Other_____

Sample Metrics

Qualitative
- Feedback
- Media mentions
- Public speaking invitations

Quantitative
- Analytics (#visitors, #views)
- Social media (#likes, #shares, #followers)
- PR successes (#appearances)

Best Practices for Getting Started

- Think of engagement and outreach efforts as opportunities to exude your executive brand.
- Pick content ideas that connect your values, beliefs, and goals with those of your organization.
- Set clear targets for how often you conduct each type of outreach and to whom.
- Include outreach activities internal and external to your organization for increased visibility.
- Stick to a few existing outreach methods rather than spreading yourself too thin.
- Stack or layer outreach efforts onto existing routines to build new habits.
- Leverage relationships with internal and external stakeholders who support you.
- Keep building.

What outreach content ideas will you commit to?

- ☐ Share stakeholder stories; celebrate their wins
- ☐ Recognize employee triumphs and tenure
- ☐ Circulate company news: milestone achievement, corporate social responsibility initiatives, etc.
- ☐ Share job openings and career opportunities
- ☐ Author and publish content about your causes
- ☐ Repost articles about your causes adding your point of view

Canvas 12: Workplace Engagement

You have crafted your EPIC executive brand in various forms and explored different approaches and pathways for outreach. When embarking on this journey, a central objective has been to build your brand that authentically represents you and is consistently experienced by others during every interaction. This is the moment to commit to yourself how you will reliably show up across the many forums at work.

When reflecting, it's important to distinguish between "doing" and "being." For example, "doing" refers to the specific actions you take, such as leading meetings, providing feedback, resolving conflict, or supporting team initiatives. "Being", on the other hand, refers to your presence and demeanor, like being approachable, confident, or calm, cool, and collected in the most difficult of circumstances.

1. List each type of workplace engagement you commonly participate in (e.g., team meetings, one-to-ones, executive presentations, cross-functional collaborations) and place each one in its own segment of the circle.
2. For each segment:
   - Briefly describe a specific challenge you have faced in this type of engagement in the past. (For example: "In past meetings, I sometimes struggled to communicate my vision clearly, which led to misunderstandings about direction.")
   - List the concrete steps you will take to overcome the past challenge and show up more effectively. (For example: "I will prepare key talking points before each meeting and ask a colleague for feedback afterward to verify my message was understood.")

TIP

Periodically refer to your concrete steps to stay on track. Consistent follow through demonstrates reliability and focus, both of which strengthen your executive brand.

Create Your **EPIC Executive Brand**

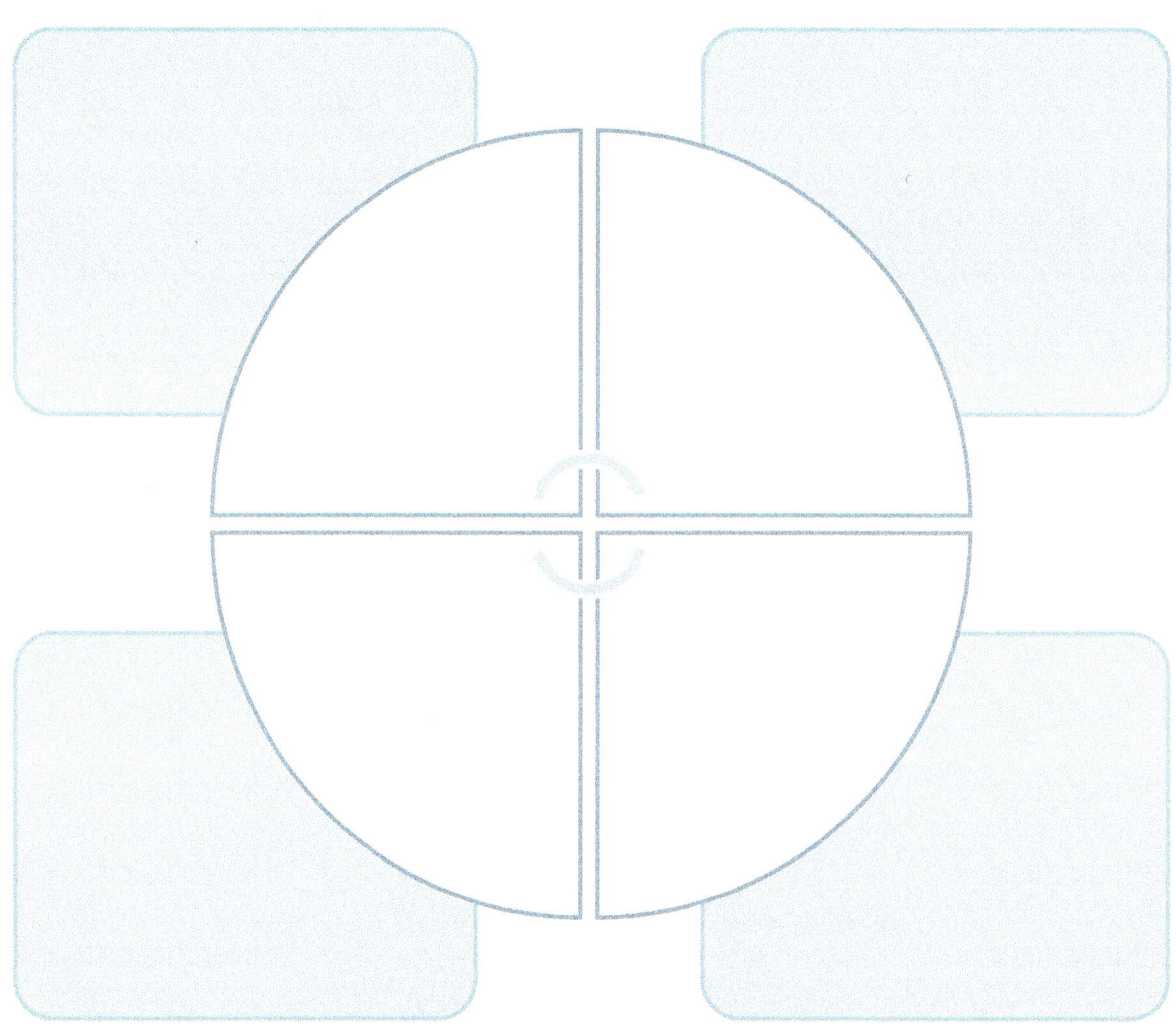

Canvas 13: Action Plan

You know what they say, a vision without a plan is only a dream.

Collect your thoughts and compose a game plan for implementation. Refer to your initial objectives to ensure you stay on track.

Your objective and timeline	Your initiatives	Your accountability partner for progress check-ins

CONGRATULATIONS

Well done! Congratulations on creating your new EPIC executive brand! Your work to Elevate your Presence, Influence, and Connectivity have the potential to heighten your career and leadership legacy.

To bring your EPIC executive brand to life, ensure it shines through every interaction. Lift and support others and remain dedicated to your cause and desired impact. Consistently connect and engage with people in your organization and industry. Doing so opens new opportunities for broadening your influence and inspiring others!

Starting new routines can be challenging. How can you stay on track? First, refer to your goals and action plans. Talk about them with a colleague who is setting out on a similar quest and encourage regular check-ins to support each other. Combine your outreach efforts with existing habits. Begin with small steps and gradually increase your activities. Identify any barriers that may hold you back and find ways to eliminate them. Reward yourself even for the smallest of accomplishments as all wins are worthy of celebration!

To support future refinements triggered by new experiences and learnings, keep all your hard work and ideas in this workbook. It will serve as a valuable resource for updating your EPIC executive brand when the time comes.

> **"Be yourself.
> As everyone else is
> already taken."**
>
> Oscar Wilde
> Irish Poet and Playwright

ABOUT THE AUTHOR & COACH

Carol Bergeron

Leadership & Organization Development Consultant | Professional, Personal, and Retirement Life Coach | Board Director | Community Leader

www.BergeronAssociates.com

As a recognized leader in organization and leadership development, Carol helps individuals, teams, and organizations turn trying transitions into triumphs. Renowned for her strategic mindset, collaborative spirit, and self-discovery coaching approach, she guides people to unlock their strengths and aspirations, navigate unique paths forward, and achieve meaningful, lasting outcomes. Over the course of three distinct careers, she has built a reputation for adaptability and resourcefulness while traversing an array of challenges.

Human Capital Champion - In the early stages of her career, Carol served as human resources leader in technology firms experiencing rapid, flat, and unstable growth. Drawing upon a background in a technology-driven family, she adeptly shaped effective talent strategies and human resources infrastructures. During times of organizational transition, her contributions were instrumental in strategic planning, business pivots, and merger/acquisition integrations.

Entrepreneur - Building on this foundation, Carol established Bergeron Associates, a consulting and coaching organization. Recognized for her track record of positive impact across life sciences, healthcare, technology, professional services, manufacturing, and nonprofit sectors, her focus is on strategic visioning, multi-generational leadership development, and professional and personal transition coaching including retirement life by design.

Eager to broaden her impact, Carol published *People Succession: Lessons from Forward Thinking Executives in Middle-Market Companies*, offering insights into leadership pipeline development. Additional works include, *Create Your EPIC Executive Brand* workbook, which provides guidance to leaders seeking to elevate their presence, influence, and connectivity, and *Take the Retirement Life Design Challenge* workbook, which supports individuals crafting modern retirement lifestyles. The workbooks augment her one-to-one and small group coaching programs. She shares more wisdom through her newsletter, *Transition Touchpoints*, empowering readers to navigate challenging transitions with confidence.

Board & Community Leader - In addition to consulting and coaching, Carol is committed to community and board leadership with special interest in advocating diverse talent and fulfillment in senior living. Notably, she co-founded the Executive Exchange program that supports the advancement of professionals in life sciences and promotes the Scandinavian model of senior care, aiming to improve wellbeing and longevity.

Carol is recognized as an accomplished leader, coach, and consultant committed to helping others navigate meaningful transitions. What sets her apart is her commitment to leveraging each client's distinctive qualities to unlock their full potential and guiding them to not only achieve but sustain long-term success.

www.ingramcontent.com/pod-product-compliance
Lightning Source LLC
Chambersburg PA
CBHW061821290426
44110CB00027B/2946